Empath

The Complete Guide to Develop Your Gifts and Find Your Sense of Self.

A Journey Through Spiritual Healing and Learn Life Strategies.

Master How to Control Your Emotions and Relationships.

By Marc Goossens

Table of Contents

Introduction

Congratulations on purchasing *Empath,* and thank you for doing so.

The following chapters will discuss the nature of empaths, ways to tell that you may be an empath, what that means for you, how to control and hone your gifts as an empath, how people can try and manipulate you, and how to heal from that manipulation and trauma.

There are plenty of books on this subject on the market, thanks again for choosing this one! Every effort was made to ensure it is full of as much useful information as possible. Please enjoy!

Chapter 1: Signs of an Empath

Are You an Empath?

It's often very difficult for us to know these things if we lack the ability to get in touch with our emotions. For some people, the ability to empathize with others doesn't exactly come easily. There are some individuals who have low empathy naturally, who struggle to sympathize with others and to show pity or feelings of companionship. For most people, this ability to empathize is moderate—the average person makes the conscious choice to empathize and feel along with someone else who they care about.

However, there is another small subset of people who may not feel as though they can control their ability to empathize with others. These people act as emotional sponges, soaking up the feelings—

positive and negative—of the people around them. Having a deeply emotional conversation with someone can drive someone in this minority to tears, or to take on the deep sadness of the conversation. These people have a very difficult time controlling and maintaining relationships because having any kind of intimate relationship with someone else can be emotionally draining for them. These people make up a very small part of the population, but they also have many special qualities and skills which, when honed and controlled, can make them an irreplaceable part of any group or team. These people have come to be called empaths.

An empath is described as an individual who has a hypersensitivity to the emotions and feelings of others. They're like a sponge to friends and family—the problems of others who they communicate with also become the problems and burdens of the empath who is listening. They soak up the feelings of other people and feel those emotions as their own. But, this doesn't mean that you're an empath just because you have a lot of empathy for other people. The difference lies in the lack of ability to control these emotions.

You may be wondering if you qualify as an empath. Here are some general criteria that might help to define you as an empath:

- You feel a lack of control over your emotions, and you feel unable to control the degree to which you connect with other's experiences—this may be the most important part of an empath's identity as that status. An empath will often feel out of control when it comes to their emotional state and how much they connect with other people. When a person confides in an empath, they might feel as though they're connecting with the person against their own will. When a person confides about a negative experience in you, and you feel yourself experiencing the same emotion afterward, you might have very high empathy, and you may be an empath. In later chapters, you will read about some strategies to overcome the difficulties that come with being an empath and overly empathizing with other people, regardless of your experiences independent of them.

- You're prone to extreme highs and lows or binges—when an empath is overwhelmed with emotion, mainly stress or anxiety or sadness from empathizing with someone else, they can go on stretches of extreme emotional highs and lows. This means that an empath can go into a depressive episode until the intensity of the stress or source of that stress subsides. They may even go on food, drug, or sex binges in an attempt to alleviate the stress that comes with it. On the other end of that spectrum, some empaths may experience panic attacks regularly or have a long manic episode where they lose focus on other priorities in their life so that they can try and get away from the point of stress. Empaths can also experience extreme fatigue and have periods of extreme exhaustion when they have a lot of their plate or are experiencing a lot of stress from themselves or from other people.

- They find relationships difficult and exhausting to maintain—if you're an empath, you might understand the difficulty of managing your communications with other people. Talking to people about their day or their most minute troubles can send an empath down an emotional spiral. It can cause them to lose focus on themselves and their own problems. They can easily become the victims of emotional neglect at their own expense—because of other people and the empathy they put into other people, they neglect themselves, and this causes other people to neglect them in turn. They become the victim because they have no way to communicate to other people that they need the attention and empathy from others that they're lacking.

If you think you identify with some or all of these traits, or you sympathize with these experiences, you might be an empath. So, what does that really mean for you? Being an empath comes with many special gifts that are often only possessed by people who are on that level of intimate emotional connection. However, many negative effects accompany the good ones—like the ones mentioned above, empaths are especially prone to extremely negative reactions to their own gifts if they don't know how to manage their feelings and relationships. It's especially easy for empaths and highly sensitive individuals to become attached to the deep emotions that are attached to their relationships, romantic or otherwise. They have serious difficulty pulling themselves away from their feelings—the feelings and the relationships that they forge with those feelings make up a considerable part of their personality.

This book is not for empaths to feel sorry for themselves—it's to help empaths hone their skills and abilities and come into their own as parts of the world. This book is for empaths to be able to really understand why they have those capabilities and to understand how to use them to their greatest potential while still maintaining their own emotional health and keeping a healthy distance from the things that could cause them to spiral. This book is about empaths and ways they can take responsibility for themselves so that they don't have to go through their lives, not knowing how to deal with their feelings. The way that other people process their emotions doesn't fit the mold for empaths, so this book was constructed for those empaths who need to process their emotions through a separate mold that caters more to the emotional and spiritual needs of an empath.

Of course, empaths have many talents and natural abilities that, for many, are worth their proneness to negative emotions and downward emotional swings. Empaths are deeply connected to nature, and they feel at home among like-minded people who are deeply compassionate and who can connect to the natural world with them. Highly sensitive people are able to sense the deepest emotions of a person in front of them—the emotions that other people just aren't able to pick on, and maybe even feelings that the very person feeling them isn't quite sure about. When the empath can hone their gifts in picking up on emotions without feeling them as intensely as they often do, they can be an incredible asset in many walks of life. In the creative fields like the arts, acting, poetry, and other artistic or expressive paths, there are many empaths who succeed and make a name for themselves in those fields because the required skills come easily and naturally to them in particular. Additionally, many empaths find their homes in the spiritual field. People who work as psychics or mystics or who make a living with divination are often empaths. The ability of an empath to pick up quickly on the feelings of others can also often queue them in to other parts of the person's life, and this can help indicate what the future might hold for them. Empaths are usually very proficient at reading other people's expressions and body language, making them sometimes seem clairvoyant in their ability to read and pick up on the physical cues of other people. While these skills come easier to some people than others, and they can be learned over time, the important distinction to be made between empaths and those who aren't classified as empaths is that an empath has a natural talent for picking up on these cues. There's no teaching these things to an empath because they don't need to be taught. Because they naturally have such an eye for people, they have a stronger foundational knowledge of how to read and pick up on the emotions of others through many different paths, including body and facial cues.

Additionally, one of the defining characteristics of empaths is that they are the world's natural peacemakers. They live to try and create harmony in the world wherever they can, and they can become incredibly upset when this harmony seems unattainable. More so that the average person, being in a setting, situation, or social circle where there is drama and emotional discord can severely upset an empath and can send them into a period of serious stress and anxiety or depression. This is one of the traits of them empath that can be very detrimental when not handled with care. If the empath never learns how to control their sense of compassion, they'll likely spend a large section of their lives giving their time and energy to other people only to receive stress and negative feelings in return. When this compassionate ability is honed, however, the empath makes an exceptional mediator who can seemingly find common ground between the most different groups of people, and bring people together naturally. Because of this, some empaths find their homes in the field of therapy or counseling. Some empaths find their calling in showing this compassion and helping to bring people together and increase the overall happiness in the world.

Empaths are often thought of as emotionally volatile people—while this isn't necessarily always false, it's a gross understatement of the value of empaths in society. While they may feel as though they've been outcasted from society as a whole, they play an integral role in keeping groups together and functioning. Think of empaths as the metaphorical glue which can make or break a social circle. Sometimes, without someone highly sensitive within a group, that group falls apart because they lack the compassion to communicate, and they cease to be a cohesive collection. With the empath there to mediate and speed up communication, the group is more likely to succeed as a social unit. Because of this job as the empath, they truly become irreplaceable in the context of a social circle. Though it's easy for empaths to fall into depressive and circular thoughts of low self-esteem and self-worth, they hold many social circles together and streamline the mediation process when two sides of a group may disagree or become aggressive. When an empath really hones their ability to mediate and calm down other people to allow for smoother communication, they become an asset to any group if they want to be productive and efficient.

Empaths are a group of people who come in many shapes and forms. If you think you might be an empath, you don't have to identify with all of these "symptoms" of being highly sensitive. Generally, consider the way that you react to the suffering of other people. If you're a fairly empathetic person, seeing another person cry and listening to their sad story may get you in a similar mood, seeing someone in such a bad place emotionally. However, if you're an empath or highly sensitive individual, seeing someone cry and having them confide their concerns in you might drive you to extreme emotional lows—listening to someone's suffering might drive you to a panic attack, a depressive episode, or a long period of emotional drainage and exhaustion. Many empaths struggle with maintaining their emotions when they're faced with a lot of stress or people who are either neglectful of their feelings or who are emotionally needy. When someone like this—someone emotionally needy from others and who needs attention and validation to function, these people aren't necessarily or intentionally malicious or manipulative—latches onto an empath as their source of validation and emotional comfort, the empath usually have a very difficult time separating their own voices from the voices of those needy people. It's harder for them than it is for other people to prioritize what they need from others instead of what they can give to others. Generally, if you think you might be an empath, you're probably compassionate to a fault. You feel the need to give and give to others, even if it's of a detriment to you. Not only are you highly sensitive to the stresses and feelings of other people, you do most anything you can to comfort them and provide for them. In addition to being peacemakers between large groups of people, you also thrive in a position where you have the power to individually help others feel better and be more emotionally stable, even if that act destabilizes you. This is one of the other defining features of an empath—because of their lack of ability to prioritize themselves, they often give to others without allowing themselves to receive the same attention and care. Many empaths participate in the mode of thinking in which making someone happy will make the other person happy in turn. Unfortunately, this mode of thinking usually only ends in the empath falling back into a depressive spiral. While it might be satisfying for an empath to service other people emotionally, it's even more important for the empath to distance themselves from other people so that they can emotionally service themselves.

This is another one of the faults of empaths—they often fall into the delusion that they can only be validated by the attention of other people. It's too often only when the empath can learn to use their own judgment instead of the judgment of others when making decisions in their personal lives that they realize this is false. Because empaths are so sensitive, they sometimes have a hard time believing that they're allowed to make their own choices. Often, the parents or guardians of an empath have something to do with these harmful patterns of thought as they grow into adults.

For example, some empaths grew up with "helicopter parents" —guardians that constantly hovered over them and, in a way, prevented them from developing a normal sense of social importance and individual importance. The helicopter parent is so focused on the well-being of their child from a physical standpoint, and keeping them safe and away from any harm or danger, that they don't let their child experience life naturally. When they don't expose their children to all kinds of situations, some bad and some good, and offer them room to grow on their own, they become dependent. Although this kind of parenting is generally bad for all children, it can be especially detrimental to empathic children who connect with others on a deeper level than the average child. When an empathic child isn't given the proper opportunities by their parent or guardian, they lack the skills necessary for them to connect and disconnect with their peers when they need to. Instead, they either grow up with the inability to connect or—more often for empaths—they find that they can't help but always be connected to other people. When they can't disconnect from others, they become dependent on everyone else around them, which can severely lower their self-esteem and confidence.

All of these characteristics of empaths culminate into a few core issues that will be addressed further into the book. While empaths have many talents that are readily available to them as long as they know how to access and properly use them, they also have many drawbacks that come with those abilities. In general, empaths tend to lack self-esteem, confidence, and independence. While this can be rectified at any point along the way, it becomes more and more difficult for anybody, empath or not, to correct this kind of thinking the older they get. Like any bad habit, more time spent before working to break, it is time that the bad habit is solidifying and becoming stronger. So, this is a call to action for any empath who understands that they might struggle to disconnect from others, heal themselves spiritually from their bad habits and detrimental thinking, or who needs a regular boost in their confidence. The work to correct these things is still difficult, but this book can hopefully inform you of ways you can work to better yourself through methods that are easy to understand and easy to implement into your daily life.

This has hopefully answered the underlying question of this chapter—are you an empath? Empaths are regarded as some of the most special people in the modern world because of their gifts and unique abilities when it comes to connecting with others—specifically their talents and natural aptitude for peacemaking, mediation, and emotionally supporting others. However, most empaths aren't born with the ability to harness, hone, and maintain those abilities, so they tend to use them without focus and without understanding that there are healthy and unhealthy ways to use their abilities. With the proper coaching and practice of those aptitudes and natural skills, the empath's skillset can become powerful assets both to an empath and the people around them.

If you believe that you are an empath, keep reading. The next chapter will focus primarily on how to keep distractions at bay and really hone in on your inner voice as a way to guide you through life as you learn more about yourself as an empath and discover how you want to use your unique understanding of people. While the path is different for every person, and no two empaths are exactly the same, many suffer from similar issues as it pertains to their particular natural talents. Because of this, it's important to properly address those issues so that as many empaths as possible can be helped on their path to spiritual healing and honing their abilities.

Chapter 2: How to Harness the Inner Voice

Many times throughout our lives, we hear and see content that involves the idea of a conscience or an "inner voice". This voice inside of us is supposed to ideally guide us toward better things and help us on the paths that we've been set on. This voice also sometimes takes the form of a cartoonishly small angel perched on our shoulder, giving us advice and guidance as we try to navigate through a confusing and often isolating world. Empaths tend to have very strong inner voices, but also often have the hardest time initially connecting with them and keeping that connection strong. When the connection to conscience is made and maintained, the bond is very strong and will serve anybody, empath or otherwise, well in life.

The inner voice is an abstract concept for many people. It can have an emotional, spiritual, or even religious connotation. Put simply, when we refer to the "inner voice", we refer to the sense of moral and conscience that is independent of other people and is unique to the person who possesses that inner voice. The conscience in empaths tends to be very powerful, so it makes sense that their innermost voice would also be very powerful. However, that power aside, it can be very difficult to control the inner voice if you have no practice in doing so and you have spent your life listening to the conscience of others instead of your own judgment. This is the case for many empaths—they listen to the opinions and voices of other people before they really get in touch with their own judgments. This can make their inner voice and conscience really weak and hard to differentiate from the will of other people.

If you're an empath, you may relate to this struggle—it's hard for empaths to prioritize their own opinions before the opinions of other people. Because of this, they have a hard time telling what opinions are their own and what opinions are just thoughts that they've internalized from listening to other people. While it isn't bad for empaths to listen closely to other people and really consider the points of view of other people, it can be a serious detriment when they don't take the time away from others to listen to their own thoughts and opinions so that they can make their own decisions. If you find yourself simply following others' commands without really stopping to consider how you weigh into the matter, you may need some practice in discovering your inner voice and how to follow it. There are a lot of different ways for an empath to really get in touch with what they're feeling on their own, separate from the feelings of other people, but one of the most effective ways for anyone to quickly practice communicating with themselves on a deeper level is through meditation.

For many empaths, meditating is a good choice when it comes to drowning out other people and listening to their own thoughts in their head. It's a good way for anyone to connect deeply with themselves and really focus on centering themselves mentally and emotionally. Meditation is perceived by some with skepticism, but the science behind it is simple. When we follow a certain general breathing pattern and learn to relax our bodies and just let our thoughts run out, we achieve a different kind of electrical brainwave. In shorter terms, meditating alters the way we think and perceive the world around us.

Because of this change, we're able to think more clearly, act more calmly, and connect deeper with ourselves and our conscience. This can be daunting, especially for individuals who find that their thoughts tend to be unpleasant when left to run rampant on their own. This is unfortunately very common in empaths in particular—the mind of someone highly sensitive tends to react strongly to negative thoughts, and the mind of an empath is more prone to snowball from there. However, it's most important to understand that having negative or intrusive thoughts during meditation is normal and not something to be concerned about. Instead, try to keep your thoughts on a tighter leash—when you find that your thoughts are running in a negative or unproductive direction, stop yourself and bring your mind back to a point of focus, like your breathing.

A simple method for meditation if you're a beginner starts with carving out a small portion of your day where you can sit down and relax in a familiar or comfortable space where you can guarantee you won't be disturbed for at least 5-10 minutes. After you've found a space and become settled, close your eyes and let your hands find a comfortable position. Focus on your breathing and let it be the focal point of your attention until you're in a calm, meditative state. Again, this focal point will also come in handy if you find that you need extra focus, or your thoughts are becoming unhelpful to your relaxation. Some people use verbal mantras like the well-known "ohm" sound as another focal point. For some people who meditate, allowing yourself to repeat a sound or mantra over and over allows for the thoughts to quiet, as the room isn't too silent. This isn't necessary, but it helps some people to find their focus quicker and more easily. Other people use a visual to be able to focus their energy, like the image of a balloon expanding and shrinking with their breath. This is beneficial for some people, but also completely optional. All of these things can serve as your chain to draw negative thoughts back to.

The point of meditation, for many, is that there doesn't have to be a point. Even though we're discussing meditation as a way to focus your thoughts and help yourself become less dependent on others, meditation is just a nice way to calm down after a long day for some people. If you want, you can just sit down and relax into a blank, meditative state—although this point of blankness is harder to reach for some people than others, don't give up!—and let your thoughts wander in and out of your head until you feel calm and your mind feels reset. This is what many people do, especially those who have been practicing for a long time. The mindfulness that meditation can help so much with is a hobby for many who meditate on a regular or even daily basis. But, for the purpose of finding your inner voice as an empath and learning to listen to it more actively, let yourself have a calm inner monologue when you've reached that calm state of meditation. Although it's important to note that you "talking" to your inner voice doesn't mean that you should treat it like a separate entity, it's alright to communicate with it just so that you can establish a connection with your conscience and get used to using it and listening to it. Remember that your conscience is an extension of your mind and thoughts, and not some higher being or different persona looking after you. The advice that your conscience "gives" you is really advice and thoughts that you probably already know to be true. With that in mind, don't be afraid of your inner voice! It's a navigational tool because it is an extension of your subconscious, so you already know the right decisions to make and the perspective that you should take on things. Never feel as fault for a poor decision if you took the time and perspective that seemed the best on the problem.

There are many ways that you can "communicate" with your inner voice while you're still in the earliest stage of establishing a connection with it. It can include self-affirmations, which is the choice for many at first. Some people choose to just mentally go over something you need to do in the day—although this isn't recommended if that thing you need to do will bring you stress and therefore out of the calm state—or something else that will let you listen calmly to the voice inside your head. Most people who utilize self-affirmations will do this by getting into a meditative state in which they can breathe and think calmly. After they've achieved this state, the person who meditates can either repeat some kind of mantra out loud to themselves, or they can simply try and let that affirmative thought occupy their mind.

There are many different kinds of affirmations that can work for many different people. It depends on what kind of connection you want to make with your innermost voice and what struggles you need that help to work through. If you need help with self-esteem or self-worth, for example, some good affirmations might be "I am enough", or "I can make my own choices". The affirmations should be short and sweet, short enough for you to repeat it rhythmically without forgetting it but long enough for the point to really be hammered home and have an effect on you. Verbal affirmations don't appeal to everyone, but anybody who wants to see an effect in themselves over a long period of time could benefit from using them. Not everyone who uses verbal affirmations uses them in meditation, either—some people wake up in the morning, look at themselves in the mirror, and say their verbal affirmation. In this case, the affirmation takes effect because it's the first thing that you hear yourself say that morning, and you ideally say it while your brain is still waking up and sticks more to information that comes into it. When your brain is still in that early-morning mode of grogginess, the conscious mind struggles to function until you wake up more. When you get up right after waking up, you're more likely to remember the first thing that happens and the first things you experience. If you make those first daily experiences positive, you'll see an overall change as you keep up that habit.

Although it may seem strange or foreign at first, the idea of listening to your own internal voice will be easier and more familiar the more that you practice. Have conversations with yourself or just hum a little tune inside your head when you can, even if it's out of your meditation time. Take any opportunity you can to be familiar with the sound and tone of the voice inside your head. After a while, you'll be able to pick out your conscience from the sound of your passing thoughts. The conscience should ideally sound calmer and more consistent in cadence, as opposed to the inner monologue of your thoughts where the voice jumps from one passing idea to another. Both of these voices are extensions of yourself, but they each serve a very different purpose in helping you and allowing you to navigate your life independently. Knowing how to pick this voice out of the passing voices of other people when it comes time to make a potentially important decision will be a very valuable asset to you.

When that time eventually does come and you, for whatever reason in your life, need to make an important decision that could affect both you and other people, being able to really separate your inner voice as a navigator in your life from the voices and opinions of other people will make your life as an empath easier. When you stand at the point where you have a decision to make, it's usually a good idea to pause. If you can, take the time that's offered to you to make the best decision you can. While it may feel like the more time you spend making the decision, the more time you're wasting, it's better to make a drawn-out but best decision than to make an unnecessarily hasty knee-jerk choice when you didn't have to.

Don't make the assumption that you should never consult other people when making an important decision or a decision that impacts more people than just yourself. While your inner voice should be the most important, and the core opinion of your own decisions, getting second and third opinions when considering your options is almost as important as being able to think independently of those other opinions. The best decisions that are made are made with the help of other people who have many varying opinions. When consulting other people, try to ask people who have made many different life experiences and are from varying walks of life. The different lives and experiences of the people you consult will lead to many different perspectives. When you have many different perspectives to consider when forming an argument or opinion, your final decision will likely end up more well-rounded and less likely to fail—the flaws of one perspective have been accounted for by the opposing perspective of someone else. Different opinions complement each other and culminate into a more intelligent argument or choice. However, not everyone should try to get these opinions from other people. If you feel that, as an empath, you can maintain and defend your own opinions against the wills of others, then it's important not to distance yourself too much from other perspectives. However, if you think your will might be too easily influenced by other people, this method of developing a choice won't work for you yet.

During the time that you take when making an important choice, if the choice you need to make affects you and not others or the circumstances are specific to you, distance yourself from other people if at all possible. You should also distance yourself from others if you're someone who feels that at the moment, you have trouble keeping your opinions from being directly swayed by someone who disagrees. While it might be important for this decision to take the opinions and thoughts of other people into account, you have the final say. So, while you should take some time to listen to other people, you should also take some time where you can completely separate yourself from other people with their own biases and agendas so that you can process your options without interference from someone else. If no one else is there with you to interfere with the way you make your decision or weigh your options, you're only real choice in that moment is to listen closely to your inner voice. That inner voice that you had hopefully been working on listening to more should now be louder and clearer than it might have been before. This makes that voice a lot easier to listen to and understand. Remember that your conscience and inner voice are an extension of yourself, but these methods of bringing out your inner voice are to help you use yourself and your own ego as navigational tools instead of the opinions of other people exclusively. Relying solely on other people for guidance weakens the soul and makes it a lot harder to make decisions. Whenever you would be in a situation where you have to make a choice on your own, you might be at a loss because of your dependence on other people. However, when you become familiar with your internal voice, and you hone your ability to listen to it, prioritize it, and follow through with its suggestions, you gain a powerful asset that no one can take away from you. After all, it's your mind and your ego talking, and no one can revoke that.

This voice should also be used for guidance not just when making important or life-altering decisions, but also when you're living your daily life. As you become closer and more familiar with your inner voice, they start becoming a part of your normal thought process as you go through your day. When you become more used to calling on that conscience for guidance, the process of calling on it becomes easier and easier every time you do it. After a while, it should be second nature to listen in to your conscience. After that, the conscience should play at least somewhat of a role in your normal life. Whether you're out for a walk or considering starting a new series on television, the conscience plays more and more of a role in our lives, the more we interact with it and work with it. When we become more focused on it, and we interact with it every day, it interacts with us, in turn, every day. This comes in handy when you're learning, as an empath, to manage your relationships and feelings in a way that doesn't hurt you or put you at risk for any kind of emotional overload. When you can get in touch quickly with your conscience and inner voice, it's useful to have a perhaps calmer, more centered version of yourself ready and able to weigh in on issues you face on a day to day basis. Whether it be wanting to drop a potentially negative or toxic friend, or what to do about a stressful situation at work or home, your inner voice should be the source of advice you turn to before you seek out to guidance of anybody else

This is one of the fatal flaws in many empaths—the lack of ability to prioritize the self and the conscience of themselves. Empaths tend to habitually seek guidance from the people around them because they're more easily overloaded by stress and other emotions than other people. While this in itself isn't subject to change, it makes the standard empath more likely to be taken advantage of and more likely to be unhealthily dependent on the validation of other people. When the empath learns to disregard the opinions of others for the sake of their own inner voice and their own feelings, they're effectively freed from those bonds of other people's expectations of them and validation. In later chapters, we'll go over how best to manage stress and deal with emotional overload, but for now, it's more important to try and minimize the amount that you rely and depend on other people's opinions. Instead, listen to your own thoughts before you ask for the thoughts of others. Other people's opinions should always be supplements or friendly challenges to your own opinions—this is how you grow as a person. When the opinions of others start to overshadow the faith you have in your own decision-making and ego, it becomes unhealthy, or codependent. It's easy for many people with low self-esteem to fall into this unhealthy and even potentially abusive cycle, but empaths and highly sensitive individuals are put at a higher risk because of their heightened sensitivity to stress and the stress of other people. As an empath, catch yourself if you think you might fall into a codependent relationship with someone around you. Never use other people or their opinions as crutches for your own—you probably don't really need the help from them. What work you might have before put into your requirement of validation from that person, you should instead put into focusing on your internal voice and acting on the advice you can give yourself.

This will be an important topic to be touched on more in later chapters—the way that the empath treats themselves when it comes to the things and voices they listen to when they need to make a decision. The status of an empath is one of their most important qualities, at least to themselves. It's very important to many empaths that they regularly act as peacemakers—it's relevant to their identity and their place in society. If an empath can't act as a mediator, they sometimes feel as though they lose all their worth as humans. Because of the way that we tend to categorize all people, especially in friend groups or social circles, we tend to place empaths in this hyper-compassionate role. When an empath breaks from this role as a more complex human being, there sometimes exists a large amount of stress over the change. Empaths are often incredibly concerned with how people view them and how much people want the empath to be around, so the empath tends to adhere to the social norms of their friends and companions. There are some empaths who can ignore this pressure and who live their lives with less social stress. However, many empaths get caught up in this role of mediator, so much so that they lose sight of themselves and their own views. When the empath is too caught up in their role as a peacemaker and the social glue of a group, they often only serve to hurt themselves in the process. Especially because the common empath is used to prioritizing others and is more prone to care more about others than themselves, giving a lot of their attention to the problems of others can be very dangerous for them. In the next few chapters, you'll learn how to manage your feelings as an empath in the world, how to take better care of your relationships, and—perhaps most importantly—how to take care of yourself. Many empaths would benefit from placing more relevance on self-care—it's an important wave in modern culture that every individual deserves to take care of themselves. This may be harder for empaths than for other people, as people who aren't so highly sensitive to stress and other people's distress have an easier time disconnecting from other people and focusing on themselves. However, this skill is one that requires more practice for empaths—it isn't unattainable to them.

In the next chapter, we'll cover ways for the empath to maintain their emotional independence from other people. This is one of the most important ways for empaths to help themselves live their best, most fruitful life. While a good first step to becoming a more functional empath in society includes interacting with many kinds of people in a healthy way, not everybody can do this right away. Some empaths just can't operate healthily with other people right away, so they first need to distance themselves from other people for the purpose of building up their self-confidence and self-esteem. This confidence has to be developed for any empath to live their best and fullest life in the world.

Chapter 3: An Independent Empath

As we've discussed in prior chapters, social independence is one of the most important things to an empath who wants to succeed in life both in terms of their personal success and their success with other people like them. While many empaths will flourish in life if they go into a career where they work in large groups, most empaths have yet to channel their ability to distance themselves emotionally from other people. This ability is one of the most valuable when it comes to an empath's ability to exist as an individual person without becoming too attached to other people or other people's perceptions of them.

Make no mistake—social interaction is one of the most important things, especially to an empath. On some newer versions of the famous scale of what every single person needs to survive and prosper in order from most important to least necessary, Maslow's hierarchy of needs, on the bottom and most basic level of requirements is food, water, shelter, and social interaction. This edition of the pyramid of needs accounts for the almost unique requirement for human companionship. Every human will die or go insane if they have to function for a long enough time without any kind of companion, bond, or interaction with another sentient being. This rule is true for any person, but it's especially true for empaths, people who thrive on social interaction despite their sometimes severe reactions to the emotions in those interactions. Because empaths cling so tightly to interactions and their bonds with other people, it's very hard for them to let go of bonds, even for their own well-being. When empaths, in particular, are forced away from their source of social interaction, they can suffer even more greatly than the average person. They suffer from a kind of withdrawal, similar to an addict. Because of this, most empaths try to find a lifestyle where they don't have to be apart from people, friends or otherwise, for a long time or entire workdays. Working in social spaces with many collaborate and group activities are perfect for empaths, for example. So, though this chapter is about distracting yourself from the group's opinion and focusing on yourself instead of other people, don't take this as advice to distance yourself from your friends and family or to shut people out. This is something that many empaths can be found guilty of—when they aren't exhausting themselves through too much engagement. They're finding ways to shut the world out so they can isolate themselves. Both of these sides of the spectrum are unhealthy and should be avoided at all costs. Rather than encouraging you, as an empath, to distance and shut yourself off from the world, this chapter should serve as a reminder to find a happy medium between those two extremes. If you can find that happy medium and maintain it for the most part in life, you will be happier because of it.

There are "symptoms", or signs that an empath is being overly stimulated in a conversation or is generally being overloaded with sensation within a social group. One of these signs is that the empath is actually experiencing common sensory overload. Experiencing sensory overload daily or almost daily, or experiencing it to a very severe degree, should be taken as clear signs that you aren't taking care of yourself and need to take a break from the amount of social activity that you might be engaging in.

Sensory overload is an experience felt by most people at some points in their life—it is felt most often by people who suffer from processing disorders, ADHD, or some kind of anxiety disorder. Sensory overload occurs when the brain is receiving too much stimuli. The brain takes in a massive amount of different types of stimuli every minute of our lives, and they filter through that amount to truly process and experience a minuscule portion of it. When the brain is overloaded, it can filter through too many stimuli at once, and the conscious mind becomes overloaded quickly. You might be able to recognize sensory overload as a feeling of your brain "shutting down", becoming more anxious or more easily agitated, feeling panicked or a strong urge to remove yourself from the situation or run away or becoming twitchy or developing twitch-like movements. Think of a time where you were at a party, for example, or in another extraordinarily busy place where it felt as though you were seeing or hearing too many things. The experience probably made you feel short of breath, panicked, or just restless. This is sensory overload. Most people will experience it from time to time.

Empaths and highly sensitive individuals, in particular, will already experience sensory overload much more often than the average person. Empaths are more likely to filter through more information and sensation when it pertains to emotion, connection to other people, or socialization. So, at least at a party or in a social circle, an empath is more likely to experience sensory overload after less time spent with a party of people. However, just because the empath is more likely to experience it doesn't mean that sensory overload should just be dealt with and looked over. After enough of the experience, any anxiety or stress in the empath will be intensified because they become even more hypersensitive to stress due to being overloaded. Empaths are already more sensitive to stress, so an added amplifier to that stress is one of the least healthy things for the empath. If you're an empath and you experience sensory overload often, you eventually develop a sense of when it's coming. One of the best preventative measures you can take as a highly sensitive person is to excuse yourself from the situation if at all possible when you feel sensory overload approaching. Just giving yourself a few minutes in the restroom or away from the source of overload can allow you to rest your mind for a short time and calm down. Letting your brain cool off for just a few minutes can allow you to usually return to the situation and continue whatever it is you were doing or had to do before you felt the beginning stages of sensory overload. If you simply let it come and go, the problem doesn't become resolved. More often than not, when people ignore their overload and just push through it, the underlying issue only proceeds to get worse and worse the more they overlook it as a serious problem. This is one of the worst flaws in empaths in particular—the tendency to overlook glaring issues in their own emotional and mental health for the sake of forcing themselves to enjoy and participate in others' company. When an average person does this, it's easy for them to become exhausted quickly from the lack of attention that they're giving themselves. So, this negative impact of neglect is amplified in the classic empath, who is especially sensitive to emotions and stress, and who is the most likely to go through a period of exhaustion after being exposed to so much stress in other people or in themselves.

Here's a way for you to learn to treat yourself better from a psychological perspective—treat your brain not as an organ inside you, but as a pet. A pet relies on you for help and assistance in everyday life, and they have ways of communicating with you to let you know what they need and how to help them achieve that need without becoming sick or injured. These same things apply to the brain, whether the brain belongs to an empath or not. When we treat our brains with kindness and take care of it as though it were another sentient creature separate from ourselves, we often end up caring more for ourselves and behind happier and healthier as a result. Strangely, humans find it so easy to neglect the brain and the body as long as they belong to us. Applying that same neglect to anyone or anything else is viewed as cruel and unusual punishment.

There are many ways in which the brain tries to deliver messages to us in order to let us know that something is wrong or that they need something from us. Sensory overload is a perfect example of this—when we experience sensory overload, our brain is taking in too much information and trying to organize all that information too quickly. So, the brain needs a moment to rest and process all that stimuli; this is the brain's way of asking for a break from us. When we ignore that plea for help, we're giving our brain even more work to do with even less time for it to rest and regenerate. The brain asks us more and more for a break or for some distance from the source of all that extra stimuli because the brain needs that distance for a little while until it catches up with the rest of us. When we give in and listen to our brain and take a break from the source of overload, we can come back to it more productively and faster. In reality, while taking a break might seem like the lazy way out, or as if we're giving up, we actually improve our brain's overall efficiency if we just listen to its signs to us and let it have a break.

On the flip side of that, sometimes our brain tries to tell us the opposite—that our break maybe has gone on for too long, that our mind is done resting and now wants to get back to a place with stimuli and people in it. When we don't listen to this sign either, bad things can happen quickly. Although companionship is one of man's most basic and primal needs because we need social interaction to live sanely, it's also a need for a physical, neurological purpose. When we talk to new people and experience new things relatively often—say, one small new experience a week and a larger new experience or new connection made every month or so—-we renew our neural pathways and allow for new pathways to be made along with those connections and new experiences. If we deprive our brains of new stimuli, those brain cells die at a faster rate. The brain is a beast that is constantly changing, evolving, and growing. So, in order to give it the proper room to grow and develop, we have to keep up with our friends and family to an extent. Communication is a must for every human at some point if they want to continue living a normal life, but there are other ways for the brain to be stimulated. Simply consuming "fresh", new media, like a book, a television series, or a video game, can help our brain stay organized and refreshed for a time. This is helpful for empaths who may have difficulty associating with others because of social anxiety, or who are simply very introverted. While more extraverted individuals may not have very much trouble going into the world and seeing new things and meeting new people in order to get their fix of new stimuli, introverts and more sensitive people might want to take that process calmly and much smoother so that they don't accidentally overstimulate themselves. Staying inside and talking to a friend or family member over the phone just to check in or catch up can be enough to tide some people over on their social interaction quote for a while, but face-to-face contact has to be made at some point for the interaction to really be as helpful and emotionally stabilizing as it can possibly be. We might receive messages from our brain that we should get out more if we feel lethargic all the time when we usually are fuller of energy. If you find that after staying home for a while, you feel depressed or tired all the time, it's your brain trying to tell you that maybe you should check up with some friends or call a relative who you care about, just to see how they're doing. This lethargy or sense of depression is caused when the neural pathways that are used to being stimulated and excited are becoming old and worn, not having been used in a while and no new ones being created at the rate they should be. Additionally, we get a rush of endorphins when we step outside our comfort zone, or talk to friends or meet somebody new. These endorphins, like serotonin and dopamine, help us feel happy and motivated so that we keep having those experiences. After a while of not going outside or not having new and beneficial experiences, our brain has no reason to release these "happy hormones", so we don't feel as energetic or easily excited. This can cause people, empaths especially, to fall into a depressive rut or a cycle of exhaustion. You don't want to get up and get outside because you don't feel motivated to do so, so you don't go outside, so you don't get that endorphin release, so you feel less motivated. Once you convince yourself to break this cycle, however, your brain will thank you and reward you with the next rush or those chemicals that come along with a new, pleasurable experience.

Listening to your brain, along with your inner voice, will help you navigate the confusing feelings that often come along with the social aspects of being an empath. On the one hand, as an empath, you find yourself naturally gifted with the ability to connect easily to other people and relate to them more quickly than just about anybody else. This makes you a great communicator, companion, listener, and mediator between people. On the other hand, you have a high sensitivity to negative emotions and influences like stress, anxiety, exhaustion, and intense sadness or depression. This means that you might have to take mental breaks from people, places, situations, or groups altogether in able to get your head and heart all on the same page. because of these warring attributes, it can be hard to settle into a comforting routine where you aren't constantly exhausted by the people you spend your time with.

Everybody on Earth gets exhausted of their friends and family from time to time. It's a natural part of the human identity—ironically, even though we place such a massive relevance on human connections and companionship, everyone has to take some time to themselves where they can be apart from even the people they love the most. Solitary activity and relaxation are just as important, if not more important, that socialization. This is especially true for empaths. As an empath, you thrive on social interaction because you thrive on the connections you build and the bonds that service you and who you serve other people with. However, you also find that you grow tired of these connections more quickly than other people might, so you need to take a break from your loved ones more often. This can lead others to believe that you're distant or cold, but the reality is that as an empath, you are simply not built to endure intense social interaction for long periods of time. Because of the way you connect with other people, you settle into the default of connecting with people quickly on an intimate level. Because of that fast and intense relationship, your emotional stamina isn't up to par with other people who might take a more relaxed approach to building relationships. While there's nothing wrong with the way than at empath builds their relationships, it makes sense that they would need breaks more often. So, when you feel like the pressure of work or social groups is getting to be too much for a little while, remind yourself to step away from it all when you can. If that means taking a week-long vacation or just spending the weekend inside instead of going out, giving yourself some time to physically calm down and allowing your brain the break it needs and deserves will allow you to return to those relationships stronger than ever. And, when your brain tells you that your break is over, listen to it and get out of bed and go outside if you can—talk to someone at the bus stop or just take a walk outside. Seeing the world around you again will bring you back to a calmer state and help you release some of those endorphins you might have unknowingly been craving. Maintaining the balance between the breaks that you and your mind deserve from the stresses of your everyday life and the moments where you need to draw the line and get outside and get back to communication becomes much easier when you just listen to your body and to your mind. These things, along with your conscience, act as your natural navigators and will let you know when they need something directly from you. Hopefully, taking a minute every day to listen to your brain and body will help you get more in touch with maintaining a healthy distance when needed, but not letting that distance linger or intensify to an unhealthy amount.

The next chapter will talk about one of the more controversial subjects when it comes to navigating life as an empath—the worst kinds of people that empaths always seem to get stuck with. These people drag you down into a circle of emotional abuse and neglect that empaths, in particular, seem to have a hard time getting out of. These people are narcissists, and they mix with empaths like oil and water. The next chapter will talk about these narcissists and how empaths can spot a narcissist before it's too late and they can avoid losing potential years of their life in an emotionally abusive friendship, relationship, or other kind of connection.

Chapter 4: The Narcissist

There are many different ways that people take advantage of others around them. If the people are at something of a disadvantage, or they're emotionally weaker, more sensitive, etc., the individual can and will find a way to take advantage of and manipulate everybody they meet who they perceive as being worth their time. Unfortunately, empaths are very likely to be victims of emotional abuse and manipulation by people who want someone around them who is empathetic or is always willing to give other people the benefit of the doubt, even when they might not deserve it. This is one of the defining features of an empath—giving anybody more chances than they should to redeem themselves. Thus, they always seem to get themselves into the most frustrating and complicated situations when it comes to relationships and friendships that turn sour.

The kind of person who is the most likely to take advantage of an empath is the narcissist. A narcissist, in layman's terms, is somebody who is infatuated with themselves and obsessed with making other people pay attention to them so they can make themselves seem and feel bigger and more important than they really are. For some reason, narcissists and empaths often tend to end up in relationships and pairing together. These relationships never end well, but the inverse personalities seem to attract. Because of this tendency, it's always a good idea for empaths to be aware, so that they can be better equipped to spot a narcissist, know if they're in a relationship or friendship with a narcissist, and understand better how a narcissist functions on the psychological and emotional level so that you, as an empath, can get out of the relationship or friendship faster without letting yourself be tugged deeper and deeper into the cycle of abuse.

Narcissists are more common than you might think. While the number of people who actually suffer from NPD—Narcissistic Personality Disorder—is minuscule compared to the general population, the amount of people who could be categorized as having a narcissistic personality is much larger. If you walk down a busy city street, chances are you would bump shoulders with a narcissist or two. Of course, the label "narcissist" then becomes much vaguer and more general. While narcissism as a trait is defined by a set of characteristics and habits, there are different degrees of narcissism—most "narcissists" we meet in our lifetime aren't the exaggerated villainous version of narcissism that we sometimes imagine in our minds. In fact, some of our closest friends and family may have some narcissistic characteristics. In general, these things are the biggest tells for a moderate to severe narcissist—the degree at which the narcissism becomes detrimental and harmful to not only the narcissist but the people around them at large:

- Lying—many severe narcissists also become or tend to be pathological liars; that is to say, they lie about even small and insignificant things to embellish their life and make themselves seem more interesting. Often, this lying is compulsive—the person telling the lie doesn't necessarily want to lie to the degree or the amount that they do, but they feel as though they've fallen into a bad habit that they physically can't break. Even though a pathological liar is someone who lies a lot and has some practice in hiding when they aren't telling the truth, everybody has some tells if you know what to look for. Most people, for example, will look upwards and to their right, or your left, when they lie. When a person looks up in this direction, it almost always means they are visualizing something or making something up on the fly. If they look up to their left or your right, they're recalling information, indicating that they're telling the truth. If you think someone you know is lying, you could tell by comparing their behavior once you ask the question to their "baseline behavior" — when someone is calm, they fidget less and maintain eye contact, so these rules are usually broken when they lie. However, this rule of eye signaling is true of most people, regardless of whether you know them or not. Additionally, many narcissists will dispute you when they can in order to assert dominance. If you explain something that happens or happens often, they might insert themselves into the discussion by contradicting you. It's possible that you both know who's right, but the narcissist is more concerned with arguing and *seeming* right than they are with actually being correct.

- Bragging—this is maybe the most stereotypical trait of a narcissist, and it often rings true for most of them. Most narcissists will brag about their lives, their looks, money, home, or whatever else they can think of to make themselves feel higher and others feel lower. The bragging and embellishment of their lives and self comes from a place of emotional trauma of their own, so they usually don't know how to communicate with other people without being rude and hurtful—they were probably never treated kindly or warmly as a child, so they never learned how to do the same to their peers. Along with the narcissist's trend of bragging to anyone who will listen, most narcissists also have severe delusions of grandeur where they think of themselves as "chosen ones", or people who are intrinsically meant for something greater. They know that people treat them differently, but they interpret that treatment as justification to their claims that they're special in some unexplainable way. Generally, narcissists just tend to believe that, for whatever reason, they were always meant for something much greater and on a much larger scale than anybody else. Whether that means they see themselves becoming a CEO or famous celebrity, or they genuinely believe themselves to be on the level of a religious figure or deity, narcissists are destined for something beyond the normal scale of greatness. To them, they've always been different from birth in a good way. The harsh or negative treatment that they receive from others because of their self-centered behavior, in their warped perception, is usually one of two things—either a challenge from the universe to test their mettle, or "haters" who are simply jealous that they'll never stack up. In either of these scenarios, the narcissist has a clear disconnect from the world around him and the people in it. The other people exist outside of the narcissist, making it much easier for them to talk poorly of the general public and see themselves as inherently better than everybody else. This is why you'll notice as you learn how to pick out a narcissist and interpret their actions, that narcissists tend to keep around large circles of people who probably really care about them. This isn't a group of like-minded people or a support system for the narcissist. On the contrary, these circles serve as target practice for the narcissist. Because they're often so set on the idea that there's something big in store for them and that they have a destiny higher and greater than anybody else's, they feel as though they need to polish their "people" skills. Those "skills" usually include the ability to manipulate and control others without letting them leave the narcissist. Because narcissists tend to have remarkably low empathy. they use more compassionate and passive people as stepping stones to get what they want because that's how their perception of the world works.

- They have a knack for manipulating others and making them feel lower than the rest of society, especially their manipulator. This might be one of the reasons that empaths and narcissists always seem to end up together—they both have a talent for understanding the feelings of others and are interested in knowing what makes a person tick. The difference lies in the reasoning behind that interest for both parties. An empath, on the one hand, probably wants to understand the people they're close to so that they can be generally closer to them and be able to help them emotionally if the need arises. For a narcissist, the intention is quite the opposite. Where the empath wants to be closer to the person, they're trying to understand. The narcissist really has no interest in "understanding" the other person on an emotional or compassionate level. They don't empathize at all with other people because they don't perceive compassion as a way to serve themselves. Therefore, they really just want to understand other people and why they feel the way they do so that they can exploit the more emotional person for their personal gain. Additionally, empaths tend to get sucked into the personal circles of narcissists because they really have a knack for building up circles of people who they use as emotional shields. When a narcissist builds up their social circle, that circle of people is really on there so that the narcissist has somebody who will listen to them and so that the narcissist has a specific victim. Not only do narcissists enjoy manipulating others, they specifically enjoy finding people who are vulnerable and knocking them down even further. Empaths are usually prime examples of these emotional targets for a narcissist. This is unfortunate, but if you're reading this book, you won't be a victim for much longer. Or, if you're someone who luckily has never been taken advantage of by a narcissist, you'll be at almost no risk of being in that kind of neglectful relationship if you just follow this chapter's instructions.

With these tells in mind, you'll be more able to pick a narcissist out in your life if they exist in it. They might be an acquaintance or friend of a friend, a colleague at your job, or even somebody close to you. Again, most narcissists we encounter are self-aware to some degree or are a mild enough narcissist so that they aren't a danger to others or to themselves. However, most of us will encounter a full-blown narcissist or two in our lives. So, it's better to be prepared than to be unequipped and accidentally roped into neglectful and manipulative contact with a narcissist.

Before we delve into how to best avoid prolonged contact or a relationship with a narcissist, we have to better understand the many shapes that a narcissist can take. If we can point out the different kinds of narcissists and how they act compared to each other, we have a better chance of dodging interaction with any kind of narcissist.

In general, narcissists are sorted by two factors, and there are three subtypes within those factors. Firstly, a narcissist can either be overt or covert. This factor is determined by whether or not the narcissist really loves the spotlight and act narcissistically through stereotypically limelight-hogging means. If they do, then the narcissist is overt. If they prefer to be more deceptive and sneakier with their relationships and partners, as well as their personality in general, then they are a covert narcissist. The other factor is determined by what they attach their special status to. Some narcissists attach themselves to ideas of beauty, physical appearance, fitness, and youth. These types are somatic narcissists. Other narcissists view themselves as special and above others because of their supposedly superior intellect. They place a heavy emphasis on the brain, mathematical and analytical skills, and being perceived as smart. These are cerebral narcissists.

The first kind of narcissist is the classic narcissist. They act just like the earlier shortlist of traits which are most commonly found in someone with NPD or who is the stereotype of a narcissist. They love the spotlight and are very rarely self-aware of their actions or the negative impact they have on others. This kind of narcissist is always an overt type because they love the spotlight and they thrive on attention from anybody who will give it to them. It's important to note that the classic narcissist is almost always more obnoxious and annoying than they are malevolent or cruel. Because they're very rarely aware of the scale or impact of their words and actions, they fail to realize how much they hurt other people. This is why this kind of narcissist is so often stereotyped as "the narcissist" —not only to they make up the perfect stereotype of somebody who simply loves the spotlight, they also make up the part of the stereotype where the narcissist is completely deluded, unaware of their actions of the way that they impact other people. This type of narcissist can be either cerebral or somatic.

The second of the subtypes is the vulnerable narcissist, also known as the closet narcissist of compensatory type. This narcissist embodies the underlying fear and anxiety that most narcissists have on the inside—they feel the need to make up for something that they lack either physically or emotionally, so they cling onto other people who have strong personalities so that the narcissist can leech off them and share a bit of the limelight that way. That being said, this kind of narcissist is always covert—they don't like to be directly in the spotlight of any conversation and are often plagued with stress and worry if they're forced into that position. Ironically, though the compensatory narcissist is much more worried about other people's perception of them than any other kind of narcissist, they are almost equally as unaware when it comes to understanding that they have a negative impact on others, especially the people they attach themselves to. Even though they tend not to be very self-aware, the closet narcissist usually places more of an emphasis on their intelligence than their appearance, making them more likely to be a cerebral type. They can be serious trouble for the people that they choose to latch themselves onto, as this type can also be very manipulative. This is the type of narcissist more likely to gaslight people who try to leave them, and who are more likely to try guilting their friends or partners into spending time with them. Though the compensatory type is much weaker in their personality, that doesn't mean that they should be glossed over or considered safer to be around than the classic narcissist. However, most people don't consider them to be the most dangerous type of the three.

Which brings us to the third type within the three subtypes—the malignant narcissist. This is the classic narcissist when we think of a narcissist who abuses everybody around them knowingly. The most aware of the three subtypes by far, falling under both the cerebral and the somatic category, the malignant narcissist is the parasite who will grab hold of you and refuse to let you go no matter what. Not only are they often experts in gaslighting, guilting, and all other kinds of emotional manipulation, they usually are more than willing to abuse the people around them psychologically or even physically in order to get what they want. They tend to be crueler and generally more ruthless than the other two types. Additionally, the malignant narcissist is the most likely of the three types to become physically violent around other people, no matter who the person is. The malignant, otherwise known as toxic, narcissist, is the only type that can be either overt or covert in nature. Some are more covert, and they use emotional and psychological manipulation to quietly keep their victims on a short leash. Others are more overt, willing to make a scene and even physically abuse their close ones in order to make a point, get what they think they deserve from them, or even just to let off some steam. Most researchers agree that of the three subtypes of narcissists, you should always be the wariest of the malignant narcissist. If you find that you might know a malignant narcissist, whether you're close with them or not, be sure to get away and break that connection as fast as you can—and consider other people who might be closer to the narcissist or who also know them in any format. Of course, you should be wary of every kind of narcissist. They can all become dangerous to you and your mental health, especially if you're an empath or highly sensitive individual, very quickly. Luckily, there are many ways that you can learn to spot any kind of empath from a mile away, and subsequently learn how to avoid letting them develop a connection with you. For many people, knowing how to cut yourself off from a narcissist is the difference between a normal life and years of emotional and psychological abuse.

The remainder of this chapter is meant to keep you and your loved ones safe from narcissists of all kinds. While not narcissists are intentionally malevolent or necessarily physically dangerous to you, all people with narcissistic personalities would benefit from learning to drop those traits and develop happier, healthier habits. When those people fail to change because they think they don't need to and fall deeper into the cycle of narcissism, that's when that individual becomes unhealthy and possibly dangerous for you to be around very much. That's why these skills are included in this book. While it's the firm belief of many that we are intentionally put through many trials in our life to prove that we are worth the good things we are given, most people could stand to dodge a few metaphorical bullets in their life. Narcissists are one of the nastiest bullets to wrench out. Like a parasite, all kinds of narcissists know just how to find your weak spots and play into them, especially if you're an empath. Some people think this is why empaths and narcissists so often end up in relationships or friendships—aside from the "opposites attract" school of thought, narcissists are naturally attracted to people who they perceive as weak. One of the weakest-sounding things to people who have little concept of the importance of empathy or sympathy is somebody with an excess of either of these things. To a narcissist, someone who gets upset at the pain and suffering of others is naturally weak and deserves to be "taught better". While this method of thinking is disturbing for a lot of people, better understanding the psychology of a narcissist is the key to, in turn, better understanding how to decrease the chance of one becoming attached to you. For future reference, think of narcissists as parasites. Some are benign at; first, some are malignant right from the beginning, but they should never be there and they always become unhealthy soon enough, with the sole plan to destroy you from the inside out for their own personal gain.

With that in mind, here are some of the things you can do to be wary of narcissists before you're even sure you've come into contact with one:

- Be wary of the way you come off to other people. It's not a bad thing to seem compassionate to other people—it's almost always a good thing—but to narcissists, this is someone who they can prey upon more easily than the average person. Consider the way you walk and hold yourself when you walk down the street or ride public transport for your daily commute. There are a few simple rules to make yourself seem more direct, bold, and confident, without necessarily seeming uptight, cold, or guarded. Firstly, be mindful of your posture overall. Anybody can tell a good amount about just about anybody by getting a good look at their overall figure and the way they stand. Stand with your feet planted firmly on the ground when it's natural—try not to cross them in your natural position. This makes you physically more stable on the ground. To be more specific, point your toes outwards instead of inwards. This makes you look a bit more extraverted. You suddenly are now more open with your stance—you look more inviting and less like you want to hide. Moving upwards, keep your back straight up when you can. Most people these days don't have fantastic posture, so a rigid back might make you seem guarded or too professional, but sitting or standing tall instead of slouching makes you seem more confident and outgoing. Moving up once more, the jaw and head matter a lot to the general "feel" of your body language—after all, this is the area that a stranger will look at first when they see you. If you want to appear more confident and bolder, avoid pointing your chin down—this makes you seem submissive and weak. Instead, face your jaw either directly out or slightly up. When we look someone straight on instead of looking at them from slightly below—assuming height is roughly the same—we show them that we consider them an equal and would like them to do the same. Looking at someone head-on is a sign of respect more often than not. When we point our chin up, we assert ourselves as the dominant one in the conversation. Where direct eye contact makes the encounter more friendly and respectful, looking at someone from a slightly upward angle makes the dynamic much more forceful and less balanced. Looking down your nose at someone is usually a sign that you view them as beneath you and intend to treat them as such. Of course, this is a more extreme version of just tilting your head up a bit. When we get more used to this posture, we tend to feel more confident in addition to acting more confident. This becomes self-fulfilling, and the perception of confidence through our own body language makes the confidence real, encouraging more of that strong body language.

- In addition to the way you actually look when someone takes their first glances at you, also take into consideration your tone of voice and word choice when you speak to someone for the first time. Of course, your word choice is part of your personality, and whether or not you want to make a large change to the way you come off to others is your choice entirely. However, be aware that some of these changes make it less likely for a narcissist to worm their way into your life. With that in mind, there are a couple things that narcissists might take note of when it comes to pointing out a submissive person in the midst of speech. For example, there are a couple of body language cues that transfer over in speech. Someone who usually talks to people with their head tilted downward will usually talk with a quieter, more cautious tone. Or, they might speak with a more uptight-sounding voice, as though they were afraid of misspeaking or offending somebody. This doesn't mean that you should never consider what you want to say and how you want to phrase it before it comes out of your mouth—it just means that being more relaxed in speech makes you seem more outgoing and makes you much less of a target for narcissists. To an extent, word choice can also play a role in this when it comes to the likelihood of a narcissist taking note of you and trying to form an attachment to you. When we speak, we choose words to make our tone more consistent. Someone more submissive might say, "sorry for making you wait", or "sorry for being late." Someone more confident in themselves and with a more dominant disposition might change their word choice and instead say, "thank you for waiting for me.". Both of these choices are polite and respectful, but thanking somebody instead of apologizing makes both parties feel better about the interaction.

Consider the last time someone has apologized fervently to you or someone you know who apologizes maybe a bit too much. When they apologize for something, whether it was really their fault or not, it still probably didn't feel very good. Although it's respectful and sometimes comforting to know a person has the presence of mind to apologize for wrongful actions, it can make everybody feel uncomfortable when the gesture becomes excessive. Instead, thanking someone for something they've done for them instead of apologizing for their own action both lifts the weight off the guilty party's shoulders and makes the receiver of the words feel more appreciated. Additionally, people tend to feel better about themselves the less they apologize and the more they're thankful. It's small changes in the daily life like these that enhance relationships as well as keeping narcissists away. Specifically, malignant narcissists enjoy finding people who are weak at heart and submissive to just about anybody around them. Because of this, someone who frequently apologizes—an indicator of low self-esteem and confidence—makes a much better target for them than someone who seems to have a secure sense of confidence in themselves.

- In general, be very mindful of most people you encounter every day. All this means is that it's better to be a little overly cautious around new people than it is to dive into new relationships with everyone you meet and potentially risk becoming an abuse victim or trapped in a cycle of emotional neglect, as many empaths so often do. When you see someone on a bus or on the street, it's not necessarily dangerous to smile and say hello. Making polite small talk is usually fine with most people you meet—however, understand where the boundaries of normal connection end. When someone you have just met has made small talk with you and just won't seem to let up asking things about you, they might not be someone you want to give all of your time to. They may be someone who wants to take advantage of your open and empathetic nature—like a narcissist—or they might just be someone obsessive. If you can, don't connect with this person or give them any noteworthy response to bounce off of. Make it clear if you don't want to continue the conversation, even if it is just small talk. You don't have an obligation to keep a conversation going with someone if you don't want to, and you don't have an obligation to explain your discomfort to someone. If a stranger is trying to get information about you or your life out of you, and they feel personally slighted when you don't give it to them, they're probably an unhealthy person to be around. More often than not, people will be understanding of you if you don't want to continue a conversation that you feel might have gone on for too long. The vast majority of people probably also don't want to continue a conversation that has gone on for an uncomfortable amount of time. The people who continue a potentially uncomfortable conversation are probably not people you want to end up developing a connection with.

- Additionally, if you want to actually try and see if a person you've just met is a narcissist, ask them a few questions and see how they react to them. For example, if you think a stranger or someone who you're making small talk with might be a narcissist, ask them about how their week or day has been and see how they answer. See how long they take to answer and see how they react to the subject of themselves. Not every narcissist will necessarily enjoy being in the spotlight or being the subject of conversation, but many types of narcissists will enjoy this shift and will be more than happy to talk about themselves. Observe the way that they talk about themselves and their life. If they go for a story rather than the programmed "I'm fine, and you?" type of response, listen to the story closely. Observe how likely the story is. A classic narcissist, in particular, will take any chance they can get to embellish their life and make their personal experience seem thrilling in comparison to yours. Listen to their experiences without egging them on with attentive questions. Be respectful while you listen, but don't give off the idea that you could listen to them forever and ever. In case you want to get away from their spiel, eventually, you don't want to build up an attachment to them or their life if you can avoid it. However, consider their story and some of the elements of it. Do their experiences seem embellished or exaggerated? One of the most classic tells of a narcissist while they embellish a story is that they place themselves right in the center of the drama. While some people might tell an amusing or entertaining story because something funny or otherwise interesting thing happened *to* them, a narcissist is much more likely to put themselves right in the shoes of a stereotypical protagonist. Instead of things happening to them, they play it off as though they had to navigate through the ordeal. Additionally, very rarely will a narcissist's story end comically. Even for the sake of comedy or entertainment, most narcissists can't bring themselves to be the butt of any joke or story. Rather than being the joking end of a story, they place themselves as the victor of one of life's many trials for them—or so they often believe. In this case, when a person seems to always put themselves in the dramatic and often romantic center of the action, they cease to become as interesting and may be a strong candidate for narcissism. In this case. It's probably a good idea to get away from them.

The next chapter will focus on the spiritual healing of the empath. Often, people don't understand much about themselves as empaths until the damage is already done. Because of this, they end up having to pick up the pieces of their life once they're out of, or sometimes in the midst of, some kind of abusive or emotionally neglectful situation. Hopefully, the next chapter can help you to heal yourself and get your life back on track successfully.

Chapter 5: How to Heal the Spirit

There are many situations that we go through in our lives, which we heal from silently, without even knowing that we heal. This happens because our brain takes control for a little while instead of our heart, and we just move on from whatever hurt us. The memory itself that our heart maintains and hurts from sometimes is the scar, but the wound itself heals almost every time.

However, most empaths need help to heal themselves from abuse and other harrowing situations that they have to go through. Whether that be a relationship they went through with a narcissist who didn't treat them right, someone else who neglected their needs, emotionally and physically, or something that they're currently going through with a narcissist or someone else who might be neglecting or mistreating them, empaths sometimes lack the abilities that other people do to heal their own emotional wounds because they're usually so sensitive to their own emotions. While someone else might face their emotions and worries and then move forward in the healing process, an empath is much more likely to get stuck in that process, unable to move forward and unable to address their emotions in a healthy way that lets them cope with their worries before moving on from them.

The problem arises not when the empath hits that emotional snag necessarily—many people have some causes for worry of hearing which they have a particularly hard time getting over and which they need extra help to move past. The problem for empaths arises when they get caught in that snag and then proceed to accept help from either anybody they come across, or nobody at all. When an empath hits a metaphorical roadblock, their sense of prioritizing who they want to help them in their lives sometimes gets thrown out the window and they move into this other mode there they don't discriminate with who they're willing to depend on. This can mean a couple of bad things for them and the people around them. If they decide to let anyone they please into their life, they run the risk of being hurt again, hurt worse by the same person, or having their fears disregarded and being thrown back into the cycle of abuse. This brings the empath right back to square one and they can feel even more lost and confused than they were in the first place. This cycle can repeat where the empath just doesn't learn to trust that person and they keep giving out second, third, fourth chances and so on until they just give up or the abuser in the relationship gets rid of them. This leaves anybody, especially an empath, with serious emotional wounds that they might never recover fully from. This can also leave them with severe trust issues and problems depending on others or asking other people for help. After they're kept in a cycle of abuse for too long, their brain has more and more trouble differentiating between people—that is to say, everyone they meet can be just another abuser to the empath, and so they shut themselves off and away from everybody else.

On the other side of that spectrum, many empaths have the completely opposite reaction when they're caught in the cycle of abuse. Instead of being too open and letting anybody help them out of desperation, they instead shut down completely and seem to accept help from absolutely nobody. This is probably just as dangerous and unhealthy for the empath. In this case, the empath still acts out of desperation for help getting out of the situation, but they don't know how to do it by themselves and are afraid of being hurt. So, they shut themselves away from the world instead and distance themselves from everybody, whether they're an abuser or a genuine friend who wants to help them. They shut out loved ones, friends and family, and the rest of the world out of fear. Of course, this fear is understandable, and a common response to repeatedly being emotionally or psychologically abused. However, the similarity between these two reactions boils down to this—the processes are the same, but the second reaction skips the step of desperately reaching out for anybody they can find. It's likely that the empath who reaches out first has had much less experience with betrayal and emotional abuse/neglect than the empath who jumps right to shutting themselves off from the world.

Each of these reactions to being abused over and over again requires slightly different approaches, either as an empath going through it or as someone on the outside trying to help someone close to you who is an empath having either of these reactions or otherwise going through a similar process of being let go or trying to escape that abusive cycle. The point of this chapter is to help both the empath and the people around the empath help to heal spiritually and emotionally from whatever cyclical abuse the empath may have been involved with in the past or is trying to get out of now.

If you're an empath and you want to spiritually heal from wounds that you've suffered from the emotional and spiritual trauma of a neglectful or abusive relationship/connection you have with a narcissist or someone else harmful to you, here are some tips for how to manage your own emotions without getting too wrapped up in them, as well as maintaining a healthy support system with your loved ones without becoming too involved or too distance from them.

- Don't ever be afraid to reach out for help—this may be the most important point to make to an empath when talking about how to get out of the mode of abuse in your own mind, even after the abuse has stopped. Though our body processes that we've stopped being hit, manipulated, or guilted, our mind remains in that state of expecting neglect or abuse for a while after the abuse is over. This is why even after someone has left a physically abusive relationship, they might still flinch when someone raises their hand or arm around them—even though on the most basic level, they've long processed that they're no longer in immediate danger from their abuser, they still expect the abuse because they've made a habit of being the recipient of that violence. In a similar way, the brain gets into habits of expecting to be emotionally manipulated, guilted, gaslighted, and ridiculed. The negative habits of the brain are often much harder to break than physical ones, and this goes especially for empaths. Because highly sensitive people are so sensitive to worry, stress, and sadness, it's much harder for them to work their way out of that kind of rut. So, if you're an empath who is still struggling to get out of a situation like that, don't give up and don't feel as though you have to make all the recovery on your own. You probably have people around you who will serve as your support system throughout the healing process, and you should use this to your benefit as much as you can. If you don't have an immediate support system around you, you can either reach out to people who care about you and whom you trust to let them know what's going on, or you can reach out to a therapist or other type of professional to help you through this. The most important thing about spiritual healing is not whether or not you can prove to yourself that you're strong or resilient, or whether you can show everyone that you can get through this yourself. The priority as you move through recovery should be whether or not you make a full recovery. If you don't put all your efforts into actually recovering from the abuse of someone else, then what was the point? Although it can be disheartening and even embarrassing to admit that you can't recover all on your own, it's a human trait to need help recovering from that kind of thing. So, don't be afraid to reach out to the people and services available to you when you feel weak or like you need help. This can be friends or family, or a therapist if you're in a position to have one. Building up a support system can be one of the most beneficial things to you as you go through the process of trying to heal, and being all alone in that journey will make the process slower and more difficult. No one wants to suffer alone, and you have the right to try and find people who can and will do what they can to help you, as long as you also put in the effort to help yourself.

- Find like-minded people or people who have been in similar situations for support. Even if you have professionals and a good support system made up of your friends and other loved ones at your disposal, most of those people might not really understand what you're going through and why you feel the way you do. So, it might be a good idea for you to try and search for people who have also been victims of emotional and psychological abuse—this is especially helpful if you find a group of empaths who have gone through that abuse. There are possible support groups physically close to you, and there are countless forums, message boards, and online support groups all over the internet that can connect you to people who know what you're going through. Through this method, many different people can heal through their shared experiences, as well as share the things that worked for them specifically, which helped them to heal faster and feel better. When we're around many people who have gone through tough times similar to us, we feel a stronger connection to them and we feel as though we're less alone in our suffering. When a group of people who have suffered through very similar means band together and help each other, each individual within that same group is more likely to get better faster and live a happier, more fulfilling life overall.

- Take some time for yourself when things get too difficult—even though you will feel better overall when you have more people to help and support you through difficult experiences, you're also more susceptible to waves of feeling stuck, useless, and depressed, even more so as an empath. When one of these waves hits, you don't have to brave through it every time. Often, we need to take a break from healing sometimes—it's a difficult workout for our brain and soul to always try to get better. Sometimes we have to let ourselves stagnate for a little bit before we get back up and at it. When you feel overwhelmed by the process of healing, and you feel like nothing will get better, it's okay to take a break. If you try too hard to heal and feel all better all at once and you try to force yourself to be happy, you defeat the purpose of trying to heal yourself in the first place. Understand that healing is not linear, and your recovery isn't either. There are days when you feel like you're making massive progress, and days, when you feel like nothing you do, could ever make you feel better. These feelings pass after some time, so be mindful of the bigger picture while you take a day or two to recover and get your spirits up again. Even if you've had a bad day, that doesn't mean that you're going to be suffering forever or that there is no light at the end of the tunnel—try to stay positive. While you take a small break, have a day for yourself. Make a dessert or eat something indulgent, take a long bath, light a candle, and get some rest when you can. You can heal in other ways while you take a personal day— self-care is an important part of healing, and it should never be taken lightly. Even something small that you do for yourself throughout the day can lift your spirits and get you back on your feet quicker than you would be if you just let yourself sit in the dark and be miserable for as long as you want. This is how people fall back into a cycle of despair and depression. Even if you're in a place where actively healing yourself is hard, do what you can to always make sure you know that you're loved, and that you will heal, and that there are people always willing to help you through it.

- Make sure you can check in with people in your support system, and people from your support system can check in with you. If you're having a particularly bad day or you're taking a small break because you feel overwhelmed by a dip in the healing process, make sure you still have some way to access and be accessed by your loved ones and other people who care about you in your support system. This includes your friends, family, or therapist. Additionally, make sure you can follow up on plans with people in your support system or cancel them. Making plans and then flaking out on people in your support system is a source of unneeded stress for both you and everyone in the support system. Therefore, if you can't make plans happen or you're suddenly not feeling emotionally ready to have a meet-up with someone in your support system/a meeting with your therapist or doctor, cancel plans and don't lead people on. This way, you have a direct line of communication and both parties have set the precedent that there's no judgment between the two parties if plans are canceled. Communication between you and your loved ones is one of the most important parts of being able to heal yourself properly—if you don't feel comfortable telling the people who are supposed to help you what's wrong/what's going on in your life, there's no proper way for them to be able to help you as much as they can. Always try to be clear about what you want from the people in your life and how they can help you the best. Also, if it makes all parties comfortable, it helps many people who are trying to emotionally heal from something if they have regular check-ups with their support system. That can be every day in the morning or evening or a text every few days, making sure that you're okay. This is a good way to make sure that everyone involved is in a good headspace and keeps the line of communication clear—honesty is key.

- Understand that healing is not linear and that a few bad days doesn't make you a bad person or a failure—one of the most important ways that you can speed up your recovery is by learning to be kind to yourself and forgive yourself of the bad things you do and the mistakes you're made both in the past and the ones you make moving forward. If you can extend kindness to yourself, you can extend to kindness and learn to love both others as an emotionally stable person who can accept a new version of themselves after they've healed from their trauma. Healing, again, is not linear and it does not happen all in one day—if it did, the trauma would mean much less. When we take a long time to heal and there are many ups and downs, that often means that when we finally do "heal" —that is to say, when we heal a significant amount, as there's really no specific moment where you've completely healed from the trauma. This is another important thing to keep in mind when it comes to being in touch with your feelings and being able to forgive yourself; you will probably never stop healing from that trauma and you may not ever be exactly the same person that you were before the trauma occurred. This is a natural aspect of how we grow as humans. Although evolution is technically a process that can take thousands or millions of years, it's a process that takes place more often on a much smaller scale. On the individual level, we grow and adapt to fit the needs of our environment. If you were in an abusive relationship or were constantly around someone who made you feel bad, you naturally adapted to be able to better handle that treatment. So, even when you come out of that negative environment, there's sometimes no way to completely reverse that "adaptation". Instead, try to focus on growing even more as you navigate your healing process. Even though some of the reasons we're never the same after a traumatic period or experience is simply that we were in a state of emotional shock/had to learn to cope with it, humans also just naturally adapt and grow on their own. The person you were last month is probably slightly different from the person you are right now, regardless of what has or hasn't happened in that span of time. With this in mind, understand that things change and we must deal with them in the healthiest way we know how. Instead of dwelling on negative circumstances and feelings that we experience, take them at face value and then move on from them. The faster that you can learn to move on from negative experiences healthily and roll with life's punches—both as an empath and as a victim of some kind of trauma or abuse—the faster you will become a healthier and happier person overall. The grand scheme of your life and the universe's plan for you is much more important than a bad day or a small obstacle that is holding you back right now; always keep your eyes on the prize.

- Renew yourself, make yourself new again as many times as you need too in order to let yourself feel okay again. Although healing usually takes a very long time, it doesn't have to be boring or arduous the entire time. In fact, there are many ways that you can make the process more enjoyable for yourself and for the people in your support system who are helping you toward healing. While self-care and taking care of yourself both physically and emotionally is a good way of speeding up the healing process, the general idea of healing from trauma is putting yourself back out there and creating a version of yourself that you want to be at, a version of yourself which is healthy and positive and attainable and then working to become that version of yourself. Do this by picking up new hobbies, entering new social circles of people who you have things in common with and who are kind and understanding. These hobbies or social circles don't need to be centered around your healing process or the trauma you went through— in fact, they shouldn't be. If you want to truly move on from that pain and trauma in order to become a new and better person, there's no reason for everything in your life to be centered around that trauma, even if it has to do with healing from it. Especially with new people and things that are happening in your life, you should try and move on to become a better version of yourself who is beyond and above the traumatic experiences that you've gone through. In the process of learning more about other things and people, get to know yourself a bit better again too. Often when we're in a traumatic situation or relationship where we suffer spiritual or emotional damage, we shut down from everyone else and from ourselves. When we come out of that trauma, it can sometimes take a while before we really know ourselves like we did before the trauma. So, when you can, find the time to be alone and think about yourself. When we're around negative people, especially narcissists, we feel undervalued and even worthless. And, in order to love ourselves again like we did in the past, we have to first relearn about ourselves properly. Think of it like befriending yourself all over again.

- Get in touch with your spirit. This is something that may appeal to you specifically, or it may not. Many empaths tend to be spiritual people, so getting in touch with their spiritual side again after the abuse is often a way for them to heal faster and see more progress in themselves and in their life. Although "spiritual" is a fairly broad term, all kinds of spirituality are things that an empath could benefit from. Whether that means getting in touch with religion, praying, or just having more of an appreciation for nature, feeling more aligned with the world around you can boost recovery and make you feel happier, as well as more appreciative, for the world and the people around you who are supporting you. Being a spiritual person can help empaths especially find like-minded people and a new hobby. Empaths are often topics within the conversations of Wicca and, more broadly, witchcraft, because empaths are so incredibly unique in their abilities to enhance emotions, heal people emotionally, and their intuitive skills when it comes to sensing stress and sadness. Because of these abilities, however, empaths are also recognized by these communities as being easy targets of people with negative energy, narcissists, and other possibly malicious people. If prayer or other activities often associated with organized religion make you uncomfortable or just aren't right for you, try incorporating meditation into your daily routine or add it to a list of coping mechanisms for when you find yourself stressed. You may already meditate often as we discussed in an earlier chapter as it pertains to finding and sharpening your inner voice—if you don't, it's a good stress reliever and helps many people to be more aligned with their soul, as well as their perhaps complex emotions.

It's so easy for us as humans, especially if we're empaths, to get caught up in our own emotions—so much so that we don't see when we need healing, don't know how to reach out for help when we finally do recognize it and have trouble along the way or understanding where to go from there. Once an empath is "done" healing—again, most of the time there really is no set day or time when you finish the healing process entirely—they often aren't sure where they should go emotionally from there and how to process the feeling of being free from their trauma and the wounds that the trauma has left in their life. The next chapters will cover some of the most effective life strategies for empaths who are ready to get their life back on track, or simply empaths who are struggling to maintain a positive relationship with their skills. Everyone needs some help at times to maintain their relationships, and this only gets more difficult the more emotional or sensitive the person in question is. So for empaths and highly intuitive people, this can be extremely difficult. Hopefully, this chapter has helped to motivate you to take some of these upcoming life strategies and put them to the most effective work.

Chapter 6: To Live the Empath's Fullest Life

It can be so overwhelming and so difficult for empaths in particular after they've effectively healed from a traumatic experience of relationship, to then be thrown into the world a practically new person. Imagine you were suddenly flung into the top rank of a new job, and you had no idea what the company's name was or what its mission was. This is effectively how confusing it can be for an empath without any guidance. Luckily, most empaths and highly sensitive have their support systems which helped them through their healing process.

The focus of this chapter is for you, an empath, to have better luck and better prospects going into the world without the open wounds of the trauma and without the narcissist or other perpetrator of that trauma with you. Or, for any empath reading who's having trouble with managing their emotions in such a hectic world to have a bit more of a grasp on some key ideas and what to do when you feel that familiar sense of overwhelming emotion.

Something that works very well for many empaths and highly sensitive people is journaling their experiences. This journal doesn't need to be shared with other people at any point—for some people, it's better if this journal or diary is kept very private. This way, it's easier to pour every emotion out into the papers before locking them away— for a lot of people, being vulnerable is very difficult after they've come out of a place of trauma or abuse, so they want to do everything they can to still maintain their guard. Even when we come out of traumatic or neglectful situations, one of the slowest things to rebuild is the individual's trust in other people. In some cases, the trust between someone and the rest of the world is never the same. So, if you're someone who feels uncomfortable sharing vulnerable information or feelings with anybody else, no matter who, it might be best to keep these things in a journal. In addition to being able to keep the journal private from the rest of the world, it's also a really good way to keep track of your healing journey and your progress through the months and years after you get out of that traumatic or abusive situation/relationship. A few years after you start the journal, you can look back at the feelings you had when you first began. If you're first starting the journal now or haven't been keeping track of your progress for very long, try to look forward to a healthier and more healed version of you in the future who can look back at your words and feel good knowing that everything turned out just fine.

Of course, a journal is something that has to be sustained for a long time for this progress to become visible. That commitment can be too much for some people, and they prefer to just keep notes to themselves whenever they feel like it—any way of written or visible documentation of your progress functions the same, and the entries don't have to be daily or weekly or even yearly. But, if you aren't a fan of this written documentation or you want other ways that you can help yourself live a more balanced, fuller life as an empath, here are some strategies developed by specialists and other empaths to help keep you centered as you navigate the world. Most of them work best when they're done more than once over a span of time so that you can become more familiar with them, but they're also intended to be very easy and effective.

One of the most effective ways to care for yourself and try to keep away the energy from other people for a little while if it's all getting to be too much is called the "zip up", a strategy from Donna Eden. This strategy is one that derives from very simple visualization, a key tactic when it comes to trying to increase the happiness in your life. For this strategy, be aware of the room around your root chakra at the base of your spine. On the front of your body, the root chakra lies just at the top of the pubic bone. Begin here, making a "zipping up" motion slowly from the top of the pubic bone to either just below the chin or over your head, depending on which you prefer. Repeat this motion as many times as you see fit. The purpose of this exercise is to get your brain in the habit of visualizing energy around you as it pertains to your emotions and the emotions of other people. When you zip up, so to speak, you work on closing up your field of energy, making it more difficult for other people's negative emotions and stresses to get to you. When you unzip, if you so desire, you allow energy back into your field. This strategy is mainly for when you feel overwhelmed or when you feel like there's a lot of negative or stressful energy around you. If you keep your defenses up too much, you run the risk of falling back into the habit of shutting other people out.

The second strategy is more vague but easier initially. Many people participate in a rule called the Law of Attraction. This law states that when you envision something in your life and visualize it consistently in your head, that thing is much more likely to come to you and appear in your life at the time you need it. Use this method in your life when you work on getting your emotions in balance. You can use a journal for this as well—it makes both the practice of it over and over and the actual effect of it, easier and stronger. For example, when you want to bring happiness into your life or want to have more energy in the coming days, take out a pen or pencil with a journal or just any piece of paper and write, "I am strong and I am going to be happier.", or "I am more energetic/I will be more energetic." Write this as many times on the piece of paper as you need in order to get the mantra into your head and memorized. Visualize yourself becoming happier in the coming days or feeling more energetic. Visualize this reality of yourself that is attainable and not as a possibility, but as something that is coming to you no matter what. Keep this vision in mind in the coming days—see how you feel and what happens to you. The law of attraction doesn't work all on its own; however—you also need to put in the effort to put yourself in a place, emotionally and spiritually, where you are ready to accept that happiness and energy. If you're emotionally stagnant and miserable, there's no way for that happiness or energy to do you any good—you just aren't ready for it in that moment. It can also help if you keep a part of your journal dedicated to the law of attraction and what you bring into your life using it. It's a powerful tool because it all depends on your energy and how you use your own abilities to bring the things you need and want into your own life.

Not only is this next strategy good for empaths, it's good for everyone. Being grounded or grounding yourself is good for anyone who struggles with anxiety or stress, or anyone who sometimes has a lot of trouble feeling connected to their own body and being in touch with themselves and their surroundings. When you suffer from sensory overload or just have a moment or day when you feel overwhelmed by your own emotions, it's good to learn how to be able to stop yourself right then and there and calm yourself down. Not only is this an invaluable life skill in general, it's especially vital for intuitive thinkers and empaths. When you feel a wave of sadness or fatigue or stress or anything in between coming on, stop yourself in that moment—just stop physically and try to stop that train of thought if you can. Take a moment, and a few deep breaths and look around your space. What can you see around you? What can you feel? Hear? What emotion are you experiencing primarily and where is it coming from. What can you do in this moment to help yourself feel better? If you can, document the answers to these questions out loud to yourself. If you can't just consider those answers and put them into action. Often, we get so wrapped up in our own conflicts that we forget to pull ourselves out of our own drama from time to time. Because of this, we can get more easily overwhelmed with just about every emotion under the sun. If you want to avoid this, be more mindful of your energy—think of your energy as an empath like a reserve tank or container. The more time you dedicate to work/school, emotional labor, etc., the more the tank drains. Try to avoid draining your tank completely throughout the day if you can do so. If you feel like you're about to be running on empty, find a place where you can calm down and recharge. If you can manage your energy more efficiently, you ultimately save a lot of time that you would otherwise be using to recharge yourself. This means that sometimes you have to stay away from some things or even some people—movies that are made to get your feelings running high, people that manufacture their own regular drama and crises, and other things that you know will drain you faster. Even though it might not always feel good to have to prioritize where you put your energy into, it's an often necessary function if you want to be able to prosper as an empath.

On the topic of things which it is better for an empath or especially sensitive person to avoid, try to avoid crowds and densely packed spaces when you're able to. This will probably save you a world of emotional trouble if you can be on the lookout for large groups of people and crowds, especially if those crowds are especially emotionally charged. If an empath wastes too much of their energy on this kind of group or on any crowded space, their reserves can be sucked very quickly. Because of this vulnerability, it's usually best to avoid densely packed areas when it's possible at all. Of course, sometimes we can't avoid densely packed areas, especially if we live in particularly urban areas or we often travel. If you find yourself running low in places with a lot of people, ground yourself with some of the questions above—those questions are used for when someone suffers an anxiety or panic attack, and they also need to be grounded in reality in order for them to start to come down from the attack. The questions are meant to draw your attention away from intrusive thoughts and onto more pressing and real issues that aren't supposed to cause you stress or unease. While you might start to feel a wave of sensory overload coming on, you can distract yourself away from this overload of emotion and stimuli and instead force your brain to focus just on one very simple question that you can easily answer. For instance, "What are some things I can see right now?" When you focus on this question, you're also focusing on looking for something you can see, another task to distract you. When you find something to look at, go into some detail about them, giving yourself another task to focus on instead of the worry that had been plaguing you. All of these descriptions offer you ways to escape the stress that might be coming over you. If you can't find ways to distract yourself in a crowded space like an airport or a crowded train car, try to find a way that you can distance yourself physically from the bulk of the crowd or the source of the sound. If you can do this, you can give yourself a pocket of air and time to calm yourself down before returning to your normal space.

For example, when you take yourself away from a crowded space to calm yourself down, take a breath in for 4 seconds, hold the breath for 3 seconds, and let the breath out in an exhale for 4 seconds. This returns your body from a state of shock and emotional overload to a more stable state emotionally. If you can do this for yourself, you prevent yourself from getting too out of control emotionally. Additionally, you can do this when you feel yourself start to get overwhelmed by your feelings or the crowded environment. Ideally, sensitive people would be able to avoid these places and circumstances altogether, but this isn't feasible given that many empaths live busy and very productive lives that require travel and meetings which involve collaboration between many different individuals.

The final, and perhaps most important point to make in the context of preserving the self, the soul, and keeping relationships calm, is simply to try and have confidence in yourself. Although this is an often cliched point to make in any case, someone with confidence will always have more success in their life compared to someone who is meek and who has no confidence in themselves or in their abilities. If two candidates apply for the same position with the same qualifications, the candidate who has more purpose to their stride and more confidence that they can offer something unique and useful to a company will always get the job first. To an extent, this goes hand in hand with the Law of Attraction. When we think to ourselves that we will receive good things because we are valuable and we have useful skills, we are then more likely to receive those good things in turn. Not only can this be attributed simply to that law, that we can manifest what is right for us and what we truly desire—it's also attributed to the psychology of other humans.

Generally, people find confidence attractive—someone who is confident in their abilities or at least appears to be confident in their abilities, is more likely to be able to provide for others and protect them from an evolutionary standpoint. In a more modern world, confident individuals are more likely to be independent and efficient—they don't need the guiding hand of a supervisor as much as someone more meek or submissive might. So, this means that if you act confident, regardless of whether or not you actually feel confident, you're much more likely to land yourself a job, or the thing that you want the most. If you can't muster up the confidence at this point in your life, no matter why or when you'll be able to, faking confidence is actually also fairly healthy to an extent. If we fake confidence, we can sometimes trick our own brains into interpreting those confident actions as real confident thoughts and emotions—we're more likely to think and feel confident when we act confidently. This becomes a cycle of self-esteem boosters and confidence where we know we can do the things we want and we're ready to take on the burdens needed to get there. Within the context of managing your emotions and keeping yourself aligned, think of your mind being on a leash. Your mind, as an empath, can often go wild and chase after unproductive thoughts. When your emotions become difficult to control or out of hand, use this metaphorical leash to reign them back in. To do this, consider negative or unproductive thoughts that often come up in your head. Whether this is "I'm not good enough/worth it", "They don't really care about me", or "I'll never be worth anything", consider which negative words are the most likely to come up when you start spiraling emotionally. When you feel those phrases pop up in your head when your emotions start to spiral or your energy is feeling drained, you know at that point that it's time to evaluate your thoughts and feelings at that moment and remedy them if possible. When you stop yourself in the midst of these negative thoughts, ask yourself—is that kind of thinking productive? If you want to change or you feel like you're never improving, consider that maybe the reason is why is because you're thinking so negatively. Try to reign yourself back in when you have these thoughts by really breaking them down and analyzing not as an emotional person, but as someone who wants to understand the thoughts and feelings from an analytical perspective.

Although it can be very difficult to master controlling your emotions, especially for an empath or highly sensitive person, it's not impossible by any means. In fact, it's the effort that's put in to master the control you can have over your mind and feelings, which make your relationship with those emotions even stronger. Controlling your emotions does not mean you have to put yourself down for having them or push them into a corner of your brain where you don't have to deal with them. The key to managing emotions is to feel them, understand them, and then let them pass. If you can do this and be a passive observer of your emotions, you can more easily manage them and use them to their fullest potential.

In the final chapter, relationships move into the center of the empath's guide to living their fullest and most happy and healthy life. While it's important to be independent of other people, it's also important not to shut people out. So, keep reading if you want to be able to master handling and taking care of not only yourself and your emotions, but also the emotions of others.

Chapter 7: Controlling and Calming Relationships

One of the most important characteristics of empaths as they're portrayed in the media is that they are expert fosterers of other people, nurturers of everyone around them, and masters at maintaining peace and order within groups. There's a strong reason for these assumptions about empaths—they tend to have a very strong aptitude for other people, maintaining peace, collaboration, and fostering emotional growth in the people around them.

However, empaths often aren't born experts in their emotional craft. Taking care of other people takes a massive amount of patience, energy, and the ability to maintain your own emotions so that you aren't giving every part of yourself up just to help others. Always remember that the first priority for an empath should be yourself and taking care of your own needs—this means that when you're low on emotional battery, you don't need to nurture others in that moment. You don't have to spend every waking, breathing moment taking care of everyone around you and trying to get everyone to be friends.

It's especially important to note this as it pertains to the part of the empath who loves to draw people together and is desperate for people to get along—not everyone is always going to be friends. There are reasons that people often don't get along, and those reasons are just as valid as the reasons you might want them to get along. Even if their poor relationship contradicts what you want from them or what you can see in them, respect their wishes, and carry on. This is one of the harsh realities that every empath has to face at least at one point or another while they do their social duties as a highly sensitive individual—peace sometimes just can't be made between two parties. Ultimately, there are some social machines that work just as well when not everyone gets along. The goal is not for everyone to always be on the same page and have the same perspective—that would be boring and would make the entire group painfully one-sided. The goal for any group should simply be to be civil and be able to collaborate in a professional manner. Sometimes, anything beyond that is out of your control and out of your realm of responsibility. Although this can sometimes be upsetting for an empath to hear, that they can't really change anything in the grand scheme of that social group or sphere, to deal with it and move on is the best move when it's available. Instead of putting your energy into a group of people who refuses to be friendly or get along, you could instead be putting your efforts into a group that is more than willing to work together and who wants to be closer so that they can be more productive and efficient. This is the case when it comes to more professional relationships and environments where the parties don't really need to get along for the project or job to be harmonious and successful—in order for success to be achieved, the parties involved only need to collaborate and be civil for a short period of time.

Not every relationship in an empath's life functions like this, however. There are other situations where the two parties are friends, a pair of lovers you're close with, family, or someone else you spend a lot of time with or who you know on an intimate and personal level. If this is the case, the path to solving the fight or schism in the relationship is usually much more complicated. If you're in a position where you feel obligated to solve the issue, it can be very messy to try and get involved in loved ones' personal affairs without taking sides or seriously damaging a relationship that isn't even yours in that process.

- Make sure that you listen to both sides of an argument before you weigh in with your opinion to try and help out. Although it's a kind gesture to put forth the effort to help people you care about with your mediation skills, it can potentially be harmful to both you and the people involved in the fight if you get involved before you know all the necessary information. Talk to every involved party more than once so that you can get the proper perspectives and information. It's very possible that the majority of the fight has blossomed from a misunderstanding or a small mistake that has exploded into something much greater without it needing to. When this happens, you can try to repair as much as you can while being gentle when it comes to taking sides. Don't use words that make it sound like you prefer one perspective over the other. Instead of only citing one person in an argument, use first-person pronouns that refer to yourself and your opinions. After all, you're supposed to serve as the neutral party in this position. But, make sure that everyone involved understands that you aren't getting involved in the argument itself—you have no bias and you want to hear out everyone who's involved when it comes to making a decision for yourself. The argument, finally, is not about you as the mediator within it. The argument exists around you and you're trying to deal in it in order to help out loved ones. Ultimately, however, the argument itself has nothing to do with you and doesn't concern you unless you get involved in your own volition. Because of this, try not to make it sound like the argument revolves around you or your opinion—this can drive off the possibility of making up if the two parties can't focus properly on their own issues and making sure that they actually solve it themselves.

- You're a mediator, but you don't actually fix the relationship. This is the job of the people involved in the argument. If they want to fight and fight until the end of the day, it's their decision, and you have little bearing on the matter. You're only serving as a mediator who wants to help repair what they can and who wants to help with the flow of communication and emotions. Beyond that, it's not up to you to be able to fix someone else's friendship or relationship. Even if you wanted to fix their friendship or relationship, you could only do so much on your own to someone else's relationship. When two people fight, they don't get back together because the fighting has calmed down—they get back together because they want to work out the problem, and they don't want to fight with one another anymore out of the care they have for one another. In this respect, you can't force people to care for each other and you can't induce the desire to make up. If the parties involved in the argument want to make up, they will on their own time. If they don't make up, then they weren't meant to make up. There's not much you can do as far as that goes.

- Be ready for a "mission" to fail, and don't let it impact your self-esteem as a person or as a mediator. Sometimes, people you care about fight, and it doesn't always work out the way that you hope. We always hope that the perfect couple we know will always be together no matter what, but this doesn't always pan out. When it doesn't shape up to be the dreamy fairytale that we had hoped for it to be, we have to be ready to accept that not as a personal slight, but just as the way that things work out. In that moment, something bad has happened and you need to process that as something that happened independently of your mediation or intervention. Just because you were involved in something that ended up failing or going sour doesn't mean that you were the cause of the failure in that case. Learn to accept that not everything bad that happens is your fault or has to do with you. It's okay to feel upset when these things happen—it's normal to feel upset when people you really care about end up drifting apart, especially if that means you also drift away from them because of it. But, understand that you will always have to face these kinds of endings to problems if you're often involved in mediation between parties. Not everything works out well and not every couple or group is meant to be the way that we hope or they hope. Instead, think of it like a new door opening for each person where this last one has closed on them both. Instead of focusing on the negative feelings brought to both you and the other people, focus more on the positive emotions that can be brought to both parties after the dust settles. Think of the freedom and the opportunity that comes with ending a dispute or argument, even if the ending isn't as picturesque as we might like.

Often the hardest kinds of relationships to mediate and balance aren't other people's, however. Though it can be difficult to know what other people are thinking and feeling and trying to help and mediate based on those assumptions, it can be even more difficult for empaths to learn how to calm down and master their own personal relationships. Whether the relationships be between themselves and a lover, a family member, or a friend, it can be very hard to understand how to master not only the way that you communicate with your loved ones but also how you manage your emotions while doing so.

There are many different sources which will tell you that there are three pillars of a good relationship, or five different pillars, or seven of the best ways to maintain a healthy relationship—there are an innumerable amount of different people with different qualifications who will tell you a slightly different story of how to maintain any relationship best and most simply in a calm and collected way while enriching your lives both together and as separate individuals. However, there's really only one most important thing to remember when you aren't sure if you're managing a relationship right or you feel stuck in a problem between yourself and the other person. As far as all your individual relationships are concerned, just *communicate.* This is genuinely the easiest and most straightforward part of any relationship, and yet so many people completely gloss over it because it's also difficult to communicate some emotions depending on the circumstances. But there will be no misunderstanding in the relationship if you make sure to communicate. There's less risk of a fight breaking out between you and the other person if both of you are able to communicate about it. Long-term relationships are much happier when they spend more time just talking about their feelings and how they can improve their relationship, communicating clearly what they want from each other and what they don't want from each other. There are different love languages that people have which determines in which way you're most affected by displays of affection. Your love language might be different from your partner's or loved ones. You would never know this if you never communicated to each other. The point to all of these different scenarios is that the power of just sitting down and communication expands over literally any possible flaw that could appear in a relationship. Anything that goes wrong in any relationship can be fixed or in some way, resolved if both parties are willing to sit down and quietly listen to each other explain the way they feel, why they feel that way, and what the other person can do to fix it. If they can do this and bridge the gap between the two of them, they can go on to do anything with their relationship and the sky becomes the limit so long as they keep up that steady line of communication.

Additionally, pay attention to the things that the other person does or says—they offer clues into their likes and dislikes, their mood, and things that might be really special to them right now. If you have a conversation and the person seems to be watching a lot of movies around one specific topic or idea, maybe invest some of your time into learning more about that concept or idea and do something to bridge the gap between you and them by talking to them about that interest that they've had. Not only will they appreciate that you're sharing an interest with them and having an intimate conversation about said interest, they'll especially appreciate that you're having a conversation with them about an interest that they didn't know you had any idea about. Even if they don't pick up on the fact that you picked up the interest from talking to them, they'll still appreciate that you've actually been paying attention to what they have to say. This is just another facet of being able to communicate clearly—letting the person know that you not only care about them and their opinion, you actually actively listen to what they have to say and why they have the opinions they do. If you can gain some insight into their opinions in a calm way, you can become much closer to them as a result of that communication.

Even though it's important to pay attention to your partner, friend, family member, etc., it's also important to let them do things for you as well. If you disregard your own needs so that you can try and care for your loved one, you close the line of communication from them to you, making your efforts for them effectively worthless. For any kind of connection to work, there has to be communication both ways, and both parties have to let themselves be vulnerable. If you want to be able to care for your partner in the best way you can, you have to be able to also let them care for you. That's the most important thing about communication—it isn't just about you or just about them. Balancing your emotions with theirs is something that takes time and effort, and it also needs you to be able to genuinely need and ask things of the other person. It doesn't make you selfish to want things or ask things of them—it makes you normal. Normal and healthy relationships function when both parties are comfortable asking things of each other because they trust the other person to be upfront and open with them about it if there's anything wrong that makes them uncomfortable or simply which they can't provide.

This is at the core of the ego for most empaths—they often have such a difficult time making it through the fact that they're allowed to enjoy things. As an empath, your purpose in life is to enhance not only other people's lives with your talents and your gifts but to enhance your own life as well. If you do nothing to serve yourself with your talent, there's very little point in having those talents at all. While it may be more morally satisfying to only service other people with those skills, humans are inherently selfish and this isn't necessarily a bad thing! It's okay to want things and it's more than okay for you to really get after the things you want! This is how you manifest the happiness and the love and balance you need in your life—not by wishing for it to happen and just visualizing it with an idle wish, but by also getting into action and doing something to make your wishes come true. While visualization is an aid, it's an aid to the action and the efforts we put in every day to achieve our deepest desires and our goals. If we can't even do that for ourselves, then what's the point of exercising your gift at all? The point of *Empath* is not to motivate you so you can serve others better and be more comfortable in the role of submitting to the will of other, more confident people. As an empath, your role on the planet is so incredibly special and you are so uniquely gifted that for you to only give it to others without indulging yourself is, in turn, denying the rest of the world some of your gifts. If you only give to others, you don't really replenish your storage of energy. When you take some of the energy and spend it on yourself instead, you get the things done that you've always wanted to do! The secret to keeping your energy healthier and flowing more freely is to care for yourselves at least just as much as you care for everyone else. The intense care you have for the rest of the world is a part of your unique gift, but you are a part of that world along with every other living creature.

As you move forward on your spiritual journey, take solace in that fact—you are combined with the rest of the universe, and there is no way for you to become disentangled from it. Even if it took you a while to figure that out—even if you didn't realize it until you read this, you are always going to be together with the rest of the universe, connected to everything else that is alive on Earth. So, give the same gifts of empathy and compassion to yourself than you give to the rest of the world in order to fulfill your best life.

Conclusion

Thank you for making it through to the end of *Empath*, let's hope it was informative and able to provide you with all of the tools you need to achieve your goals whatever they may be.

The next step is to learn even more about empaths and your gifts and to keep moving forward on your spiritual journey.

Finally, if you found this book useful in any way, a review on Amazon is always appreciated!

Printed by Libri Plureos GmbH in Hamburg,
Germany